香港國際詩歌之夜 2013
INTERNATIONAL POETRY NIGHTS IN HONG KONG

編輯 Editors

北島 Bei Dao

陳嘉恩 Shelby K. Y. Chan

方梓勳 Gilbert C. F. Fong

柯夏智 Lucas Klein

馬德松 Christopher Mattison

葉覓覓
Ye Mimi

目錄 Contents

1 蛾在腋下產卵，然後死去

總有一天／ 雨不是濕的路不是平的草是不乾的傘
是不壞的／ 天空折毀／ 沙灘和海浪絕交
／ 微風露出細齒／ 雲比霧愛笑
每個人就／ 住進一座自己的電話亭／ 亭口養一隻狗
／ 或孔雀／ 或貓
每十四天發一袋硬幣／ 半個月一瓶芳香劑
／ 頭髮剔成碟形／ 必戴黑色墨鏡
冬天穿雨衣／ 夏天穿泳衣／ 涼鞋尺寸沒有規定
／ 襪子顏色傾向蘋果的／ 綠

一個人打電話給／ 另一個人／ 另一個人
打電話給另一個人
／ 就這樣不停／ 傳話下去
最後一個人終於打電話給／ 第一個人／ 總有
一天
他説／ 喂／ 第一個人也説／ 喂
他説／
他説／ 昨晚／ 蛾在我的腋下產卵
／ 第一個人説／ 喔
然後死去／ 他來不及説
／ 就掛斷電話了／ 他們都掛了

每一年的端午節／ 大家交換彼此的電話亭
／ 帶著各自的貓／ 或孔雀／ 或狗
一陣騷亂過後／ 他們摩擦彼此的身體
／ 敲打電話按鍵／ 合奏一首波蘭舞曲
／ 這是唯一的節慶

你是誰／ 她問
我是瀑布／ 他回答／ 十分虛弱地
你是誰／ 她驚／ 異／ 對著話筒／ 又一次問
你知道／ 瀑／ 布
有聲音的布／ 可以覆蓋並阻絕／ 一切
／ 像鋼琴蓋／ 水溝蓋／ 或者鍋蓋／ 那樣
／ 他回答／ 又一次
我愛你／ 她説
他淹沒她／ 急速

密閉的電話亭／ 玻璃是透明／ 如同坐在汽車裏的心情
／ 毫不費力的穿梭／ 相互滲透的風景
他們製造如紙屑般飛揚的話語／ 從嘴巴飄進耳朵
／ 從耳朵積聚在心底

總有一天／所有人說盡所有的言語／對所有人
任何誇大的比喻
和貧乏的修辭／任何漫長的牢騷和愛意
那麼／所有人就會／捏著電話線深深的螺旋
／揮舞剪刀卡嚓／卡嚓／分離話筒和話機／同一時
間裏

這時／就要發給每個人蕃茄汁／和蓬勃的歌詞
／作為雋永的獎勵

那首歌是這樣唱的
／喔／什麼都別說
／喔／誰都別和誰／攪和
／我們都要張開胸鰭／痛快過活
／什麼都別說

他們都願意唱
／唱完就罵一句／※○&＊◎
／一句／小小聲的／ㄍㄢˋ
音色像橄欖／甘美而／不髒

總有一天
／蝴蝶是不規則的矩形／駱駝長出丘陵
／橋比蛇陰鬱
／螞蟻比子彈強／而有力
每個人就／住進一座自己的電話亭
／說盡所有的言語／像高速旋轉的／果汁擠壓器

／含著風鈴的噴嚏

A Moth Laid Its Eggs in My Armpit, and Then It Died

One day there'll come a day / when the rain will not be
   wet / the avenue uneven / the grass undry umbrellas
unbroken / the sky bent out of shape / a day when sand
   and surf have gone their separate ways
/ the breeze unveiled its fine-tooth milk-teeth / and
   clouds have it all over fog for puttin' on a happy face
then everyone will / move into their very own phone
   booth / keep a puppy at the welcome mat /
/ or a peacock / or a cat
and every fourteen days they'll get a bag of coins /
   every fortnight a can of air freshener
/ have their hair cropped back just like a serving dish /
   don a pair of dark rimmed glasses
trench coats in winter / swimwear come summer /
   sandal size unspecified
/ their socks inclining toward an apple / green

someone calls up / someone else / and that someone
calls up yet another someone
/ and so it goes / from one someone to the next

until that last someone rings up / the first one / day
there'll come a day
he says / hey / says he / hey yourself
says the other / hey
last night / he says / a moth laid its eggs in my armpit
/ O / exclaims the first one
and then it died / he didn't have time to add
/ before he hung up the phone / and left them hanging
high

when the Dragon Boat Festival [a.k.a. Poet's Day]
comes 'round each year / they'll all trade phone
booths
/ take their cat / their peacock / or their puppy /
and when they've finished going at it tooth and nail /
they'll all rub up against each other
/ and play a polonaise / with the ring tones on their
phones
/ thus they'll pass their one and only holiday of the year

who are you / she says
waterfall / he answers / listlessly
who *are* you / she says / beside herself / in a maze / mint / as she directs her question into the phone
you know / water / falls
with a sound that cuts off and clamps down / on the whole kit and caboodle
/ like a piano lid / a pot top / or a manhole cover / that kind
/ he says / all over again
I love you / she says
he drowns her out / *prestissimo con brio*

in an airtight phone booth / made of glass / you feel as though you're sittin' in a limo
/ absorbing the scenery and being absorbed in turn / as you're effortlessly carried on your way
the conversation they fashion cascades like ticker tape / out of their mouths and into their ear

/ canals and forms a little heap in the cockles of their
hearts
one day there'll come a day / when everyone'll have
exhausted all discourse / repeated every puffed-up
metaphor
to everyone they know
every tired turn of phrase / every long-winded
grievance and expression of affection
that is when / they'll / twist their phone cords into a
corkscrew spiral
/ and in one fell swoop / flourish their scissors snip /
snip / off with their handsets!

that's when they'll get a Bloody Mary / and the lyrics to
a thriving song
/ in a gesture of recognition they'll savor forever

and the song will go like this
/ O / don't you say a thing

/ O / don't you have a fling
/ for when our fins take wing / we'll make the rafters ring
/ so don't you say / O / don't you say a thing

and everyone will want to sing it
/ and when they're done blurt / ※○&✻◎
/ i.e., a single / barely audible / *frig'n!*
with a tone like an olive / divinely / dirt-free

one day there'll come a day
/ when every butterfly will be a lopsided carpenter's square / every camel sport a hill
/ every bridge throw on an air of gloom more fearful than a viper
/ the ant will be mightier than the bullet / more powerful
then everyone'll / move into their very own phone booth

/ and there they will they will discourse all discourse /
like a high-speed / juicer

/ mouthing a wind chime's hatchoo

(Translated by Steven Bradbury)

2 她冒汗的左手是冒號的

那是第 7 天/ 她在小島邊緣享用早餐\ 太陽是吼著的/ 草海桐像一隊潦草的引號與括弧\ 她冒汗的左手是冒號的
那些㊣梅花鹿的眼睛無論如何都是愛是和煦的海洋\ 很容易就可以把牠們擰乾
酥脆的時間像蘋果派/ 不斷有人把羊挪開剩下牛

大家都需要睡美人與哈巴狗
就像港口需要船溫泉需要蛋
監獄發給他們鎖

珊瑚礁石留在原地等海歸來
她的皮膚浸成一種陽光黑\ 天空是鏡子藍/ 林投是啞巴綠\ 所有的□□/ 都可能被□□□沖泡成夏季的西瓜奶
中午過後/ □□經常變得肥沃

在/ 風的指紋裏她找到3顆\ 鹽

她發呆的樣子是夜裏的觀音洞

Her Perspire-y Left Hand Was Semi-Colon-y

That was the 7th day / she was savoring her morning
meal on the edge of the isle \ the sun was growly /
nau-
paka shrubs were like a line of slipshod quotation
marks and brackets \ her perspire-y left hand was
semi-colon-y
the eyes of those certified ㊣ sika deer no matter how
you put it are love are warm and genial seas \ so ease
-ily / wrung dry
crisp time like apple strudel / people are forever cutting
the sheep from the cattle

everyone needs a Sleeping Beauty and a pug
like a harbor needs a boat a hot spring a thousand-year-
old egg
the prison issues handcuffs and locks

coral loiters in the place from where it came waiting for
the ocean to come back
her skin soaks into a kind of solar black \ the sky is
looking-glass blue / thatch screw pine a deaf and

dumb green
\ every one of the □ □ / could find themselves shlushed
by the □ □ □ into a watermelon frappe of a summer
season
midday over / the □ □ turn fertile fairly often

in / the fingerprint of the wind she stumbles on 3
grains of \ salt

her vacant look is the Grotto of the Goddess of Mercy
after it grows dark

(Translated by Steven Bradbury)

3 越車越遠

她蒐集各色空瓶，醃泡不同年份的黃瓜。按時用星期七的碎沫澆花。家裏有牛，有男人和硯台一枚。常常在院子裏打斜線。有時不小心跨過一些貓臉。爆炸也無所謂，就算鍋子裏有狗吠。喜歡寫蟲卵般的字，一粒一粒地寫。肚子裏養了一碟嬰兒屑，像玻璃彈珠那麼豔。

有一天，他們給她拉來一條鐵軌，教她在頭頂噴煙。

於是她就車起來了。對著鐵軌，對著屋簷。

我很精密。我很淘氣。我是地心引力。

她唱。

如何不被疲累？

誰在誰的邊界？

她唱。

車過窗下的時候，她的男人在窗裏望她。

手裏握著一節交流電。

他垂著臉，像是貨櫃裏的老肉桂。

她的牛在窗裏望她。她的硯台在窗裏望她。

牠們困惑極了，不斷從眼睛擠出墨汁與奶，

滴滴答答。

寂寞比水甜一點。
魚比海還酥綿。
從此，我就要去荒原荒原。
她唱。

她越車越遠。

The More Car the More Far

She amasses all manner of colored jars, cucumber
marinade of varying vintage. Punctually waters the
flowers with Sunday's froth. In this house there is a
cow, a man and a stone for grinding ink. Often strikes
a slanted line across the yard. Now and then capers
across some Cheshire cats without really meaning to.
Explosions are all one to her, even if there's barking
in the pot. Likes to write larvae-like words, larva by
larva. In her belly she raises a saucer of baby debris, as
brilliant as marbles.
One day they drag a railroad track over for her, teach
her how to belch black smoke from her fontanelles.
So then she cars up. Facing the track, facing the eaves.
I am precise. I am naughty. I am gravity.
She sings.
How can we avoid being bushed?
Who is at the boundary of whom?
She sings.

As she drives by below the windowsill her man is at the
window watching her.

Hand grasping an alternating current.
He makes a long face, like a shipping container full of
cinnamon gone stale.
Her cow is at the window watching her. Her inkstone
is at the window watching her.
They're so perplexed their eyes ooze drops of milk of
ink.
Drip drop tick-tock.

Solitude is somewhat sweeter than water.
Fish are crunchier on the outside, softer in the middle
than the sea.
From this day henceforth I will go forth and wilderness
the wilderness.
She sang.

The more car she is the more far.

(Translated by Steven Bradbury)

4 汗都被留在那裏了

你的咖哩裝在別人的盤子裏　名字簽在別人的故事裏
當你醒來　他們早已習慣黑暗　哼著黏牙的流行歌曲
有人在隔壁浴室洗手　把香皂握成一條魚
他咬下的那顆柿子　比獅子還金
天氣這麼寒冷　約會的地點就在太陽麻花田
她說新年快樂
他覺得無聊　只好抽煙
一隻鬼在黑板樹下瞌睡　小貓在肚子裏罰跪
我們覺得尷尬極了　從嘴裏吐出一層海
海的皮膚極白
事情並不如牠所想的那樣　也並不如牠所想的這樣
她要風　他就發給她風
他要火　她就發給他火
她們在迂迴的巷子裏勾指頭　密謀
後天　它會和同伴從紅色郵筒相約經過
最好就一起把它們綑綁　資源回收
如果妳覺得疲倦　請用複音口琴吹奏我
牠忽然渴望背著書包　脫光衣服在路上走
後來他帶她過橋　途中經歷一座廟
跟小黃瓜一樣清脆　他們的額頭

假月亮懸浮在空中

他摩擦她的眼睛　擦出一段傷　汗都被留在那裏了

And All the Sweat Is Left There

Your curry is on someone else's plate   name
    inscribed in someone else's story
when you wake   they will have long grown
    accustomed to the dark   humming some syrupy
    pop song
someone washing their hands in the bathroom next
    door   squeezes their soap into a fish
the persimmon he bit from   is more golden than
    lion
and when the weather grows this cold   they agree
    to meet in sun-twist fields
she says Happy New Year
but he is bored to pieces   and has to have a smoke
a ghost nods off beneath the blackboard tree   in a
    punitive gesture the kittens are made to crouch in
    tummies
we are mortified   at vomiting a layer of sea
the skin of which could not be whiter
things are not as it imagined they would be   nor are
    they like the other way it had imagined them
she wants the wind   so he dispenses wind

he wants the fire so fire she dispenses
the girls hook their pinkies in the crooked lane
hatch their secret plots
day after tomorrow it will rendezvous with its
familiar in the red mailbox as agreed
best to bind them up for recycling
if you're tired my dear please play me with a
tremolo harmonica
it longs to bear a book-bag on its back walk naked
down the avenue
later he escorts her across the bridge and midway
experiences a temple
crisp as a cucumber their brows
mock moonlight hangs suspended in air
he rubs her eyes rubs out a storied welt and all
the sweat is left there

(Translated by Steven Bradbury)

5 盲目約會把他荒廢

背景是鹹酥的碧綠。他們的憂傷都井在一起。一些
櫻桃變成玻璃。
她的右手像蘇打餅。擴散的指紋在空氣裏低鳴。

春天被撐開的時候\ 他們正盲目約會\ 他手裏握著一陣雷\ 她閉上眼睛像是一個空位\ 有人彈響音樂\ 有人端來焦糖咖啡\ 有人遞送黑夜\ 他輕輕捏出紫白的雷印\ 她覺得寂寞好美好滋味\ 決定繼續把他荒廢

A Blind Date Makes Him Dilapidate

The backdrop was a salty crisp deep green. Their gloom
welled into one accord. Some cherries turned to
glass.
Her right arm smacked of soda cracker. Proliferating
fingerprints puled in the air.

Now that Spring's propped up and filled to bursting
\ they're plump in the middle of their first blind date
\ he clasps a clap of thunder in his hand \ she closes
her eyes like a vacant space \ someone is playing music
\ someone is carrying a caramel latté \ someone is
delivering the night \ he deftly pinches up a purplish
white thunderprint \ she's come to feel that solitude's
so beautiful so savory \ she decides to prolong him in
his dilapidated state

(Translated by Steven Bradbury)

6 他度日她的如年

他聞起來就像一瓶沙士
她畫餅他的充飢他度日她的如年
他是寂寞的複數
她的門閂是酸
富庶的相反是他
（他們會不會幫她蓋一座九層塔？）
她頭髮他的胸膛他晴朗她的情郎
有一天大家都會變做土壤
他海過一艘船
她山過一個夜晚
星期三喜歡下雨
他們被雨織成神仙魚
眼睛被拆成謎語
然而他躲在她的鐵皮裏
靠著時間的椅背
慢慢發明一種敲打

他越是太陽她越是月亮

His Days Go by the Way Her Years

He smells like bottled root beer
her pie in the sky allays his hunger and his days go by
  the way her years
he is a lonely plural
her door-latch is sour or sore
the au contraire of plentiful is he
(won't they help her build her tower of basil?)
she hairs his chest he heartens her sweetheart
one day every living soul will turn to soil
he ocean fleets a vessel
she mountain passes a night
Wednesday likes to rain
by rain were they woven into angelfish
eyes unfolded into riddles
yet he steals beneath her iron skin
and leaning on the chair-back of time
gradually invents a kind of knock

the more he is the sun the more she is the moon

(Translated by Steven Bradbury)

7 我錄她

那天的月亮好圓，全世界的落葉都被掃到左邊。

「還疼嗎？」我問。

「一點點。」她說。

她用眼神濾掉一些茶葉渣般的陰影，嘴巴緊閉，像含著兩條鋼硬的鐵絲線。

幾隻斑馬從我們的腳邊竄過，牠們的步伐裏藏著一種遼闊的慈悲。

「有時候我覺得自己根本是平行四方。唉，我覺得我快要被搬走了——」

她皺了一下眉，說。

「被誰？」我問。

「一些聲音——」

「厚的？還是薄的？」

「那些聲音，像百頁豆腐。」

「喔？」

「每一個音孔都往我的肉裏扎——」

她的臉色蒼白，整齊平直的瀏海彷彿晾掛在雪地裏的黑布幔。

我想再問些什麼，可是那些話語不知怎地堵住了，無法從舌尖彈出。

「它們多半是晚上來，一直一直扎我、搬我。很霸氣。」

她的語調哀愁。

「多久？」我終於順利擠出字。

「三分鐘？十七分鐘？半小時？還是九小時？我不記得了——反正它們就是硬要來搬我。它們絕對是從某個人的頭殼裏跑過來的。」

她停頓了一下，又補充：「每個人的頭殼裏，多少都存放著聲音，有的甜美，有的邪惡，你知道。」

我抬頭看了一下月亮，還是跟地球一樣圓。

「被搬走會怎樣？」

「就很難回來了。」

「唉——」我深深嘆了口氣。

「你可以幫我嗎？」

「怎麼幫？」

「把我錄進這裏面。」她從衣袋裏掏出一隻紫色錄音筆和耳機，交到我手中。

「啊？」我吃驚地望著她。

「錄進去之後，它們就找不到我了——」

「那，那跟被搬走有什麼差別？」

「至少我知道自己在哪裏啊，不是被亂搬。」

於是她緩緩躺下，我扭開電源，把錄音筆對準她微微張開的嘴巴。

一些奇怪的氣音從她的嘴裏彈出，她的神情肅穆，好似一頭不斷噴氣的母鯨魚。

當氣音不再噴彈時，她迷濛的雙眼也就慢慢闔上了，她一動也不動，像是睡著似的。

我變得有些懼怕，不敢檢查她的呼吸，於是戴上耳機，按下播放鍵。

起先，我只聽見有人來回摩娑象棋，然後是滴滴答答的水聲。

鍋鏟碰撞。玻璃杯。鐵捲門。

貓叫。火。鞋跟。

每一段聲音都猛然蓋掉前一段，音量也時大時小，毫無章法。

就在我打算放棄、切掉電源時，她低啞的嗓音，突然在我的耳邊擴散開來。

「欸欸，別關，我已經在裏面了，謝謝你——」

無止無盡的落葉，持續被風掃到我的左邊。

I Recorded Her

The moon was so round that day. The whole world's
fallen leaves had been swept off to the left.
"Does it still hurt?" I asked.
"A little," she said.
With a glance she filtered away shadows like tea dregs,
her mouth shut tightly, as if sucking on two iron
wires. Some zebras scuttled past our feet, their step
concealing a kind of expansive mercy.
"Sometimes I feel I am square. Oh, I feel I'm about to
be carried off ...,"
she said with a wrinkle of her brow.
"Carried off by whom?" I asked.
"Some sound ..."
"A heavy one? Or a light one?"
"A sound like *baiye* tofu."
"Oh?"
"Each sound hole penetrates my flesh ..."
Her tidy, straight bangs hung over her pale complexion
like a black, cloth curtain over snowy ground.
I wanted to ask her more, but somehow the words
got stuck. They wouldn't spring from the tip of my

tongue.

"They mostly come at night, continuously penetrating me, moving me. They're so aggressive." Her tone was sorrowful.

"For how long?" I finally squeezed out the words.

"Three minutes? Seventeen minutes? Half an hour? Or nine hours? I don't remember … anyway, they come insisting on moving me. They definitely come from inside some person's mind."

She paused for a moment and then added, "Everyone keeps some sounds in their mind. Some sounds are sweet; some are wicked. You know."

I looked up at the moon. It was still as round as the earth.

"What will happen if you are carried off?"

"It will be difficult to return."

"Ahh …," I let out a deep sigh.

"Could you help me?"

"How?"

"Record me into this." She took headphones and a purple recorder from her pocket, placing them in my hands.

"Oh?" I looked at her, surprised.

"Once I have been recorded in it, they won't be able to find me …"

"But, but, how is that any different than being carried off?"

"At least I will know where I am. I won't have been carried away arbitrarily."

She lay down slowly. I turned on the power and pointed the recorder toward her slightly opened mouth.

Some strange breathing sounds shot out from her mouth. Her expression was solemn, like a female whale continually spraying out air.

Once the breathing was no longer spurting out, her misty eyes shut slowly. She was motionless, as if asleep.

I began to feel a little afraid, not daring to check if she was breathing. I put on the headphones and pressed play.

At first, I only heard someone shuffling checkers back

and forth; and then, the *drip, drip* of water.
Pots clanging. Glasses. A metal, rolling door.
A cat's meow. Fire. Boot heels.
Each sound cut off the previous one, the volume going up and down without any pattern.
Just as I was about to give up and cut off the power, her low, hoarse voice suddenly spread into my ears.
"Eh, eh, don't turn it off. I am inside. Thank you …"

The leaves fall endlessly, and keep getting swept to the left by the wind.

(Translated by Todd Klaiman)

8 養西鬼

現在大家都流行養西鬼了　那是一種傍晚5點到7點
出沒的鬼
這種鬼不但喜歡面朝西邊　肚皮上還橫插了一根竹
棍子
這種鬼通常很醜　可是醜得很有格調　越醜的西鬼
越受大家疼愛

每天5點她們相約在第5街的郵局55號窗口
打開那箱限時專送的西鬼包裹
撈出一隻隻暈眩的西鬼　然後緊緊牽牠們的手
她們牽著西鬼去酒吧找酒鬼玩
一堆西鬼和一堆酒鬼划拳　像是某種寵物聯誼會
當西鬼開始抽拔肚臍的棍子時　就表示餓了
大家得想辦法弄來幾桶香油和葡萄柚
讓西鬼張開鼻孔慢慢嗅
有時她們從報上剪幾篇醜聞給西鬼讀
有時她們唱幾支餿掉的歌
直到西鬼逐漸脹大　變得和紅皮沙發一樣溫暖飽滿
所有人就起立關燈鼓掌

有人提議給西鬼維他命C

有人說應該為牠們訂做新衣
有人想帶牠們上山去溯溪
有人渴望和西鬼生育
不過這都違反了嚴苛的西鬼保護條例

鐘打7下時
最不醜的那隻西鬼最快消失　最慢消失的是最醜的
　　那隻
大家都感到萬般不捨心情參差
只好原地解散等待下一次

Keeping a 西鬼

Nowadays it's popular for people to keep 西鬼
a kind of ghost that disappears and reappears from 5 to 7 every night
This kind of ghost 鬼 not only likes to face west 西
but also has a bamboo stick across its belly
This kind of ghost oftentimes is very ugly 醜 but it's a distinctive style of ugly The uglier the 西鬼 the more it's loved

They meet each day at 5 at post office window 55 on 5th street
They open the special delivery 西鬼 package
They pull out dazed 西鬼 one after another and string them tightly along by the hands
They drag the 西鬼 down to the bar to hang out with the drunks 酒鬼
A bunch of 西鬼 and a bunch of 酒鬼 playing drinking games like a pet-owner association
Whenever the 西鬼 starts to pull the stick from its navel it means it's hungry
Everyone must work to gather barrels of sesame oil and

grapefruit
to allow the 西鬼 to open its nostrils and take in the
smell
Sometimes they clip scandals 醜聞 from the paper to
show to the 西鬼
Sometimes they sing putrid tunes
until the 西鬼 swell up and become as warm and
plump as red, leather sofas
Everyone will stand, turn off the lights, and applaud

Some people suggest giving the 西鬼 vitamin C
Some people feel they should have new clothes made
for them
Some people want to take them into the mountains to
walk along the stream
Some people long to have children with the 西鬼
But these violate the strict 西鬼 protection regulations

Whenever the clock strikes 7,
the least ugly 醜 of the 西鬼 disappears the quickest
the one that disappears the slowest is the ugliest

Everyone feels upset having to let go
So they disband to await their next meeting

(Translated by Todd Klaiman)

Translator's Note:
The Chinese character for ugly 醜 is composed of the characters 酉 (5–7 pm) and 鬼 (ghost).

9 發生過的就會繼續發生過

對\ 是發生過\ 是這樣子沒有錯\ 過去的我有過去的手\ 過去的手誤解過去的鎖\ 過去的鎖像一隻黑白小陀螺\ 原地打滾等待發落\ 不斷縮回的是過去的手

沿著死生的節奏\ 我們都還會留下更多古董\ 更多均衡的坑洞\ 廢墟\ 哀愁\ 與更多馴良的蜜蜂\ 對\ 那些\ 這些都發生過\ 豔麗的很快就會變醜發臭\ 對

你還記得幾則繁複的迷夢\ ?

對\ 就是那裏\ 燈色暗紅\ 雨水雄厚\ 她的吻從你的腹肌溜過\ 對\ 我們都來自子宮\ 對\ 不住皇宮\ 對\ 有人潛好深的水\ 對\ 有人攀上高峰\ 對\ 有人辦公有人冬烘\ 對\ 有人被動\ 有人打零工

可是\ 一台電視如何讓一百個頻道同時放送\ ?
可是\ 一個人如何度過春夏秋冬春夏秋冬\ ?
是不是\ 每一雙球鞋都有它們奔跑的理由\ ?

他\在黑暗裏校正顏色\一些細微的聲音炸彈起來\對\他想起一個名字\石頭般的名字\不對\是雞卵般的名字\不對\鹽粒般的名字\不對\海浪般的名字\不對\是齒隙般的名字\對\一個他愛過的名字\對\不對\對\一個女孩的名字\他們曾經一起踩過陰天的草原\對\是發生過

對\那名字\對他發生過
對\過去對我們都發生過\對
我們\在記憶的頻道裏切換春夏秋冬
我們就是\球鞋奔跑的理由

昨天的風是不是今天的風\?
今天的你能否聽見明天的我\?

每個人\都是一座神秘的小宇宙\沒有誰能夠被誰複製穿透\她有她的沙漠\你有你的白晝\我擁有一滴頑強的墨\對\是發生過\我們都被這樣發生過\就像冰冷的插頭尋覓\溫熱的電流\發生過的就會繼續發生過

That Which Has Ensued Will Continue to Have Ensued

Yes \ it did ensue \ that's it it is true \ a former me has a former hand too \ a former lock which the former hand misconstrued \ that former lock like a top with a black and white hue \ rolling in place waiting for the sentencing cue \ pulling back nonstop is that former hand too

Following life and death's tempo \ we hold on to even more curios \ even more balanced hollows \ ruins \ sorrows \ and still more docile bees \ True \ those too \ have ensued as well \ beautiful soon turns ugly and begins to smell \ true

Do you still remember how many convoluted pipedreams there were \ ?

Yes \ it is just there \ the lantern's deep red color \ rainwater solid and strong \ her kiss slips away through your abdomen \ yes \ we all come from the womb \ yes \ don't live in the emperor's room \ yes \ some people dive in deep water blue \ true \ some people climb tall peaks \ yes \ some people administrate and some people compensate \ yes \ some people are dispassionate \ some people investigate

But \ how can one TV play 100 channels at once \ ?
But \ how can a person pass four seasons and four
seasons \ ?
Does \ every pair of sneakers have its own running
reasons \ ?

He \ adjusts the color in the darkness \ some tiny sounds explode \ yes \ he thinks of a name \ a stony name \ No \ it's an eggish name \ No \ a salty name \ No \ a wave-like name \ No \ it's a cracked-tooth name \ yes \ a once loved name \ yes \ No \ yes \ a girl's name \ they had trod upon an overcast prairie together \ yes \ it has ensued

Yes \ that name \ for him has ensued

Yes \ to us the past has already ensued \ yes
We \ use the channels of our memory to switch
 between the four seasons
We are \ the sneakers' running reasons

Is yesterday's wind today's wind?
Can today's you hear tomorrow's me?

Everyone \ is a mysterious cosmic land \ no one can be
copied and seen through by another's hand \ she has
her own expanse of sand \ you have your own daytime
land \ I have ink with which to make a stand \ yes \ it
did ensue \ We all have thus ensued \ like an ice-cold
plug looking for \ warm electricity to flow through \
that which has ensued will continue to have ensued

(Translated by Todd Klaiman)

葉覓覓，台灣詩人，東華大學創作與英語文學研究所、芝加哥藝術學院電影創作藝術碩士。以詩錄影，以影入詩。夢見的總是比看見的還多。每天都重新歸零，像一隻逆流產卵的女鬼或鮭魚。著有詩集《漆黑》與《越車越遠》。

Ye Mimi is a Taiwanese poet and filmmaker. A graduate of the MFA Film Studio Program at the School of the Art Institute of Chicago, she is the author of two volumes of poetry, most recently *The More Car the More Far* (Taipei: Garden City Publishers). A bilingual chapbook of her poems was recently published by the Anomalous Press in 2013 under the title *His Days Go by the Way Her Years*.

出版 Publisher
香港中文大學出版社 The Chinese University Press

封面影像 Cover Image
北島 Bei Dao

出版日期 Date of Publication
二零一三年十一月 November 2013

國際書號 ISBN
978-962-996-629-4

香港國際詩歌之夜 2013 International Poetry Nights in Hong Kong 2013
主辦單位 Organizers
香港中文大學文學院 Faculty of Arts, The Chinese University of Hong Kong
香港浸會大學文學院 Faculty of Arts, Hong Kong Baptist University
香港科技大學人文社會科學學院 School of Humanities and Social Science, The Hong Kong University of Science and Technology

合作夥伴 In Partnership With
英國文化協會 British Council

協辦單位 Co-organizers
時刻文化 Moment Communications
香港中文大學出版社 The Chinese University Press

贊助 Sponsors
香港兆基創意書院 HKICC Lee Shau Kee School of Creativity
中國會 The China Club
周凱旋基金會 Chau Hoi Shuen Foundation

Printed in Hong Kong